rescue

and redemption

Poetry inspired by the T. S. Eliot poem
'The Love Song of J. Alfred Prufrock'

A Love Poetry Trilogy
Book 3

Frank Prem

Publication Details

Published by Wild Arancini Press
Copyright © 2020 Frank Prem

All rights reserved:
No part of this publication may be reproduced, stored in a retrieval system, or transmitted in any form or by any means, electronic, mechanical, photocopying, recording or otherwise, without prior written permission from the publisher and author.

Title: *rescue and redemption*
ISBN: 978-0-9751442-9-9 (pbk)
ISBN 978-1-925963-03-8 (e-bk)

Even in the nether places
love.

Always, love.

Contents

about a love poetry trilogy	1
rescue and redemption part 1	7
blather	9
yesterday (never does)	11
the flickering (stilled)	13
(at least) I will know	16
again (a little) again	19
(perhaps) what my belief	21
rescue and redemption part 2	23
a brief sojourn (in rain)	25
score (for an evening)	27
in this life (nevermore)	29
a façade (of me and you) on the street	32
un-alone (au revoir)	34
thoughts of you (through cheap red wine)	36
rescue (and redemption)	37
beyond the blue (a chance)	40
words (not today)	43
by feet (into smoke)	45
the question is	47
alive (is what you feel)	49
before the day (becomes old)	52
fleet (in corners)	54
wondrous wondering (and art)	56
stealing (a kiss)	58
what (feels real)	60
we pursue	62
dances (too)	66
a tortoise (that is new)	67
existentiality (as startled in the night)	69
elation (two times)	72
too suddenly	74

watching the gold	76
used to be (then curled up)	78
as much as is needed	80
back (into grey)	83
well done (the day)	85
for everything	86
white face (and rhyme)	88
novel advice (my darlings)	90
time and hands (in the river)	93
holding on (to questions)	96
ocean (time)	98
of rock pools (and responses)	100
you and me (at three o'clock)	103
a breakfast taken (deshabille)	106
the dregs say (it is time)	108
more (the same) like you	110
original project response	113
source materials	115
author information	119
coming soon	123
other published works	125
what readers say	127

about

a love poetry trilogy

Rescue and Redemption is the third of three collections of poetry written for *A Love Poetry Trilogy*.

The origin of this work goes back a number of years to an occasion when I was fortunate to participate in a project that involved individual poets located around the globe.

Each poet chose a phrase from the body of a distinguished poem written long in the past, and used that phrase as inspiration for a piece of new poetry. New and old were then hyperlinked together to create an interactive work.

Over the course of the project three poems (and their poets) were chosen as source material for the experiment:

Amy Lowell – Madonna of the Evening Flowers (1919)
Walt Whitman – Leaves of Grass (1855) Parts 1 and 2
T.S. Eliot - The Love Song of J Alfred Prufrock (1915) (Epigraph plus Stanzas 1 – 5)

To the best of my knowledge no trace remains of the original project, but I was recently inspired to revisit and to continue an exploration of the effects these wonderful poems might have on my own work.

Each source poem commanded its own identifiable voice in my responses, and here I have worked with the Eliot poem.

My experience of this poem was that Eliot's *Prufrock* is a journey in search of love, perhaps with a companion, or for a companion. Often into the less salubrious places.

It is a poem of massive scope, with the epigraph at the beginning serving, for me, the role of Requiem. The relevant sections of the poem follow.

The Love Song of J. Alfred Prufrock

S'io credesse che mia risposta fosse
A persona che mai tornasse al mondo,
Questa fiamma staria senza piu scosse.
Ma percioche giammai di questo fondo
Non torno vivo alcun, s'i'odo il vero,
Senza tema d'infamia ti rispondo.

Let us go then, you and I,
When the evening is spread out against the sky
Like a patient etherized upon a table;
Let us go, through certain half-deserted streets,
The muttering retreats
Of restless nights in one-night cheap hotels
And sawdust restaurants with oyster-shells:
Streets that follow like a tedious argument
Of insidious intent
To Lead you to an overwhelming question …
Oh, do not ask, "What is it?"
Let us go and make our visit.

In the room the women come and go
Talking of Michelangelo.

The yellow fog that rubs its back upon the window-panes,
The yellow smoke that rubs its muzzle on the window-panes,
Licked its tongue into the corners of the evening,
Lingered upon the pools that stand in drains,
Let fall upon its back the soot that falls from chimneys,
Slipped by the terrace, made a sudden leap,
And seeing that it was a soft October night,
Curled once about the house, and fell asleep.

And indeed there will be time
For the yellow smoke that slides along the street,
Rubbing its back upon the window-panes;
There will be time, there will be time
To prepare a face to meet the faces that you meet;
There will be time to murder and create,
And time for all the works and days of hands
That lift and drop a question on your plate;
Time for you and time for me,
And time yet for a hundred indecisions,
And for a hundred visions and revisions,
Before the taking of a toast and tea.

In the room the women come and go
Talking of Michelangelo.

T. S. Eliot – 1915

rescue and redemption

part 1

blather

> *S'io credesse che mia risposta fosse*
>
> *If I but thought that my response were made*

how could I explain
the truth

my truth

so at odds
with his

sometimes
I feel that I
have lived
too long

too
over long

and the words that form
inside my mouth
are ancient
understandings

the times
have changed
and he
has no ears to hear
such sentiments

and so
I mumble
crumbs
of now stale
cake

dry

difficult
to swallow

until
one of us
must turn away

heart filled
with
mis-
understandings

and we wonder
each of us
alone

what
just happened

he believed
my answer
was so much cant
and
so much blather

I believed
with all my heart
that I wished
to be heard

by him

this once

this
last time
that I
can love him

yesterday (never does)

A persona che mai tornasse al mondo

To one perhaps returning to the world

here's to you
my darling

here's
to you

ever since you left
I have found myself
secluded

cotton-woolled

alone
in a darkness
of my own making

I could do
this

or
I could do that

I could
so many
many
things

other than hide away
as I do
in the darkness left
behind you

for a time
I hoped
that you would come back
to help me fill the world
around me

for a time
I thought
that yesterday
lived on

it never does
and nor
did you return
into this world
of *I*
alone

here's to you

here is
to darkness

here
is me

the flickering (stilled)

Questa fiamma staria senza piu scosse

This tongue of flame would cease to flicker

always
the flame has danced

I
have danced along
inside

the flickering
is a sign
of life
a-glow

to dance within
is a sign that reads
alive

that reads
living

it is the soul
I speak of
here

the soul
that is the spark

it is the soul of me
and the way I know
I am one
with all

with
everything

but the flame
is staring
now

the flame
is still

frozen
in mid flicker

no more
tremoring

no more dance

and I
am staring

and still

I
hold no
flicker

and find the flame
gone cold

a sculpture
in colours
correct

the shape
perfect
in contour

but frozen
as my soul
is frozen

empty
of all warmth

RESCUE AND REDEMPTION

I glance around

all else is blue
and white
and shadow

(at least) I will know

Ma percioche giammai di questo fondo

But since, up from these depths, no one has yet

I will say no more
of reasons

madness
is its own
cause

and ever
there is more to find
more
to draw upon

to deploy

and if I did
well
what now
can I tell
to explain it

I grant myself
one respite

only one
that must
suffice

and that is
that I drew away
before completing
execution

each of us
carries
sorry wounds

each of us
not really
healing

each
building moats
and walls
and stately barricades

to weep
behind

and hide
within

to nurse our losses
and begrudgements

my room is small
now

enough
for me

no more
the expansive
the welcoming
the hearty

you must knock
three times

you must rap
a score

you must call my name
aloud
to the heavens
and
at my entryway

I shall not
come

expect no
response

but know that
at some point
I will hear

should you approach
eventually
I
will know

again (a little) again

Non torno vivo alcun, s'i'odo il vero

Returned alive, if what I hear is true

each night
I die
a little

that is the way
the blackness
takes me

un-moving

un-stirring

un-living

only breath
to show I breathe
still

only heart
to know I bleed

I stay the night
not really knowing
there will be
a morning

and
I do not come back
alive
at all

I do not
come back
better

I come back
my mind too full
of all the things I know

of all those things
I know

and I hate the truth
for what it knows of me

I hate the truth
and what it may
reveal

and I hate
the certainty
that I have died
a little
and yet

I will die again
once more

(perhaps) what my belief

Senza tema d'infamia ti rispondo

I answer without fear of being shamed

I only
ever
wished him good

I only wanted
the sweeter things

the better

perhaps though
I came
too close

it may be
that I grew
too large

and possibly
I failed to understand
my own
intentions

but I tell you
as my answer
that I meant him well
and wanted
only
to share
a few steps
upon his way

oh
it may be
in truth
the steps were mine
not his

perhaps
I can admit
that perhaps
I needed
more
than I could say

and
perhaps
I did not know
the power
of my spoken words

perhaps
it was those alone
that smote him

never mind
what I thought
that I
believed

rescue and redemption

part 2

a brief sojourn (in rain)

Let us go then, you and I

would you walk

the day is
un-inviting

sending messages
that tell
of better things
indoors

the rain
is a drizzle
unabated
since the middle . . .

yes
the very middle
of the night

but
if we must
and
if you would
well . . .

a moment

I will retrieve
my hat and coat

my gloves
and boots

so

let us go
then
you and I

shall we sombre
along the path
endeavouring
that our feet
remain dry

or will we
as children
splash and clamber

determinedly
ignoring the sagging damp
that jewels our hats

or shouting
puffs of air
as smoke
that we are breathing

all right
then
I am ready now

let us start
at least
with hand in hand
and well prepared

to catch
one drop each
on outstretched tongues

a laugh
at the beginning
of this
our sojourn

in rain

score (for an evening)

When the evening is spread out against the sky

walk with me

let us stroll
in coats
with deep pockets

so that
when I hold your hand
there will be room
for two

we will push . . .

gently push

a hole
into the gathering grey
until
a moment
when the horizon opens

and the evening
spreads itself
against the sky

the last rays
of sunlight
coloured red

and shaded pink

will linger long
into the twilight

your hand
and mine
will share a pocket

our steps matched
so
for length
of stride

woollen caps
pulled down
over our ears
to keep them warm

my breath
exhaled
and yours
will write the score
of an evening song

to rise
so sung
into the night

in this life (nevermore)

Like a patient etherized upon a table

I roam

my footsteps
stamping
across the world
that is my self

everything
is new

everything about me
pristine

I am not that man

I am not that
was

I am not
the caricature of
me
lying comatose
as though anaesthetized
upon a table

I am
new man

I walk
new walk

I am rediscovered as
quite adequate
to all my own needs

and I can stride
my stage

I can breathe my air

I can sweep the universe
with a glance
and leave it
gleaming

I am not
yesterday

a year ago

the child that was
in a once upon
a long long time
ago

come and take
a new hand
step out into
the new day

take a look
through these
my eyes
at the world transformed

born again

I am quite
born
this time
again

and as the day parts
for me to pass
I know . . .

I know
I will never be
the man
I was

RESCUE AND REDEMPTION

never more
in this life

I
will
be me

a façade (of me and you) on the street

Let us go, through certain half-deserted streets

through
descended darkness

loitering
between streetlamps

the night speaks
step
by step

in echoes
rebounded from the walls
of sundry buildings
wearing
genteel façades

we go
through vacant streets
deserted
with the sun

one fades

the other
disappears

until only we
you
and I
are left
alone together

as we have always been

speaking
to the night
in footsteps
and the tread of shoes

the only voice
a subtle distortion
of ourselves

a façade
of footfalls

an echo

un-alone (au revoir)

The muttering retreats

and so
the day unfolds
inside my head

the voices
at their ease
at last

the muttering
retreats
and I
am left alone

brief moments
falling like a firm blow
of friendly solitude

a sojourn
away
from the perilous

a moment
of
myself

solitaire

and I recall . . .

so briefly
I recall the man I was
when it was only
you and I

I recall
but
truly that is
a *once*

a
was

and now I am
encumbered
by myself

alas
I guess
my moment
is past

the voices surge
once more

so long
old friend

my dearest
dear

until
I surface
from the depths
of me
again

thoughts of you (through cheap red wine)

Of restless nights in one-night cheap hotels

toss
and I turn

awake in the night

I should sleep
I should
close
my eyes

but there is no rest
there is
no
repose

there is only
restless nights
in a one night
hotel

cheap
red wine
into
another darkness
passing
while I think
the same thoughts
over

and over

of you

rescue (and redemption)

And sawdust restaurants with oyster-shells

I am seeking you
within the hubbub
and the burly

trying to gauge
location
by the strength
and timbre
of your voice

rising
and falling
even as you rise
and fall

blows delivered
and blows received

companionable stumbles
to the floor
of this sawdust restaurant
where discarded oyster shell
lies ready
waiting
to slice a knee
or flay a hand

so
where are you
now

high
or low

I stop
to listen

hear
only braying bellows
above the pianola
as I weave
myself
to avoid the worst

it is not
so far a night
of knives
nor yet of guns

mouths and words
fists and knees

boots

there

I hear you again

still shouting
happy

now

now is the time
to seize you
in the grip
of a firm coaxing
of
more pleasure

improved liquor

better company

better fighting

yes
better fighting
at this point in the evening
is an attractive
proposition

for myself

better air
and the chance

the small chance
of a personal
redemption

beyond the blue (a chance)

Streets that follow like a tedious argument

follow me

a moonlit
night

catch a meteor
or
a comet

they fly and fly
the geminids

come
follow me
among them

get on board

and let's explore
beyond
our atmosphere

beyond the tedium
of streetlights

and bitumen
as black as one
already misplaced
argument

instead
we can look down
on blue

we can marvel
at what
we have left
behind

and remember
what it was
when
it was great

wonderful

come
follow me
beyond our star

let the solar system
languish
while we seek
the new

a place
where we can fall in love
again
with life

re-formed

where tomorrow
is not yet
touched
or spoiled

perhaps
there could be
a chance
beyond this blue
for us to start
again

over again

over

again

words (not today)

Of insidious intent

I cannot write
for you
today

I apologise

I regret

there is no
insidious
intent

no
no

it's just
I cannot place my fingers
on a pen

cannot express
my mood
or feeling

I am
distracted
within myself

and I can find
no word

if I could write
why
I would tell you

of the balm
that comes
with thinking about the words
that I might write
to tell you
of . . .

well . . .

of everything

of anything

of all the things
I think
when I am thinking
about you

my muse of letters

but not
today

I am empty
noting only
a little sunshine

a modest breeze
that ruffles
in a pleasant
passing way

and certain rays
fallen on my face
to warm me

but
not today

I have no
words
for today

by feet (into smoke)

To lead you to an overwhelming question . . .

perhaps
a tendril in the air

hovering

smoke
on the breath
of a morning

deep
in the winter
where the white
folds high

as
a snowdrift

an unsullied
sheet

to be written upon

penned
by the feet
of a mouse

leading on
to
a halt

they are
suddenly
gone

maybe
into the air

and you
have been led
by the subtleties
of air
and mouse-pen
to contemplate . . .

an overwhelming
question
lies waiting for you

to unravel
the mist
until
comprehended at last
and released

like smoke

a tendril
in air

the question is

To lead you to an overwhelming question . . .

it will take
just
a step

just one small step
and you will be
on the path

with me

we can walk
or run
or
fly a kite

we can
hold
each other's hand

swing along
arm in arm
just
to try it out

a path
sensation

perhaps remarkable

yes
perhaps remarkable enough
to overwhelm
by you
stepping
on to my path

holding my hand

flying
even if
it is just a kite under a sky
that has been painted
a kind of blue

an overwhelming
blue

isn't that
the question

alive (is what you feel)

Oh, do not ask, "What is it?"

I will lead
into
the emotion

let it wash me
until
I feel

until I
am this thing
and
know it

set it free
to know me

I will
transport myself

I will be taken
away

I will
be
as one
saturated top to toe

oh

oh

no no now
do not ask me
what is it

do not say
this
is unwise

step
to me
one heartbeat
at a time

step to me
with faith

believe in me
when I tell you
yes

trust me
to show you
the way

allow the feeling
to take you
wave
by wave

let your emotions
confirm
what is true

close eyes

RESCUE AND REDEMPTION

open
mind

let your imagination
go

let it run wild

laugh
oh laugh

is this not heavenly

laugh
and laugh

this
is being alive

do you not
feel
alive

before the day (becomes old)

Let us go and make our visit

before the day
becomes
too old

before
my mind
finds itself
wandering to other places

and before I decide
a different course
that I might prefer

let us go

let us make
our visit
while a kind thought
still remains

and while
the serenity
of ordered rows
and fresh cut grass
might yet remind

for she loved
the garden

the sun that comes
with spring

and tended
each of her flowers
personally

too sharp
the thorns
yes
but
what is a rose
if not

beauty
has a price
and
she is gone now

so
let us go

while sun
is in the sky

while the clouds
are light
and drifting

we can follow
the breeze
that leads all the way
to that place

only
for one
small
moment

come

before the day
grows
too old

fleet (in corners)

In the room the women come and go

I find myself
a stranger
left
to my own device

inhabiting dim corners
of the room
where women come
and go
to rhythms I have not yet
discerned

my time
is a mystery

and certainties are not
available
to the passing likes
of such
as I

the time it takes
for my instant
to pass
is much the same
as the sway
this way
then that
of a skirt *en-swirl*

and the touch
so fleeting
of florid lips

yet
extended in time
by memory

to endure as
perhaps
a reason
for why I
was

wondrous wondering (and art)

Talking of Michelangelo

maybe
I should seek
my fortune
any other where
than here
but this . . .

this
is the place I know
to be
and to
explore
my most foolish
profound notions

to talk
of this and that

tomorrow
and
tomorrow
still to come

who can tell
where it might
fall

perhaps here
among you
my friends
would be just as well

to speak
of *us*

of all the moments
that held our
what might be's

as well
I know
to talk of
when we become . . .

all of us

the small da vinci's
of some new art

the paint

the pottery

the lute

the wings . . .

another
cup of coffee here
now
please
for
I must consider
this
some more

let us drink it
black

and let us tell
in wondrous words
of being
michelangelo

stealing (a kiss)

The yellow fog that rubs its back upon the window-panes

it creeps
it steals
it slithers

covers
like a blanket
fallen

familiar . . .

too
familiar

it reaches
to touch you
close . . .

close
like a lover

rubs its back
against
a window pane

then swirls
into curls
of mesmer

a cold
soft
kiss
and you are breathing it

in

you are breathing it

out

exhale

and it is a risen drift
of grey

into the air

what (feels real)

The yellow smoke that rubs its muzzle on the window-panes

oh
hush now

the beast remains
without

rubbing a yellow muzzle
on the window pane
it seeks
to capture your attention

to draw your eyes
toward

.
.
.

what

a trail
of something
that was tainted smoke
adrift

up
into the sky

like the flight
of an imagined thought

an imagined
what
might have been

if only . . .

but
it is gone

truly gone

leaving behind it
only the smudge
of a huffed breath

a fog-smear
across the glass
to confirm that something

some thing
truly
was there

it
is gone now

so very gone
yet
the huffing
felt real

we pursue

Licked its tongue into the corners of the evening

shall we pursue
it

this thing
that suggests our names
then runs

leaving a hint

only a small hint
of laughter
in the glee
that lingers in air
we both must pass through

it is a curious thing
and I
do not understand it

nor you

nor you
no

come then
after it

let us track it
and hunt

we can follow the trail
into and out of
places it has tasted
with that suggestive tongue

through every corner
of the evening
come with me

come with me
I feel my appetite
for this
rising

I *hear* it
near now
and singing

a bawdy song
for drinkers

a dancing song
to throw away
false
inhibitions

it makes my feet
skip and jump
and leap
as we pursue

I see you
from the corner of my eye

you
are dancing a little
too

and we run
in time together

footsteps
on the street
as we chase
some elusive elemental

at each corner
I can see
the way it paused
for a while

peered into
the darkness
then shimmied
away
with the night

just out of reach
and just
beyond
my touch

and your touch

but oh
this pursuit is
almost enough

holding hands
and running
with just the vaguest goal
in sight

but perhaps . . .

what if . . .

you
and I
might catch our glimpse

one glimpse
and a thing
to aim for

come run with me
come

let us pursue it

to see

dances (too)

Lingered upon the pools that stand in drains

if I dance
will you
dance

outside
in the darkness
broken by moonlight
filtered
through a drift of clouds

lingering
on the pools of dark water
that dream still dreams
in front of drains
on the street

where I dance

where you dance

come
let us
you and I
just dance

across
and on
within
the lingering light
enticing

that dances
too
upon the dreaming pool

a tortoise (that is new)

Let fall upon its back

before our approaching footsteps
love
like a tortoise
discomposed
has fallen
upon its own back

legs waving
helpless and unknowing
as we approach

each of us
from our own path
and place

neither knowing
until

until

then
at once
it begins its movement

fresh breeze
to
typhoon

and the colours
whirl

and I
do not live
on this planet
any longer

I exist
in some other place

some other
plane

and you are
an *always was*
for me

an *is*

nothing remains
that is not
new

I hold my breath
and spin
around myself

you
stunned soul
the heart of my pivot

an old tortoise
I
wave my arms
my legs

helpless

I
we

approach

existentiality (as startled in the night)

The soot that falls from chimneys

the startle
in the night was
this time
caused by a sound

it woke me

left me wondering
at the source

internal . . .

external . . .

within
or without

it has been a still night
and there is no disguise
available
to deflect
the passing wind
no

a trickle
of sound
as of rain
made fine
but solid
has played patter pit

has woken me

a slight startle
only

but bringing
a sense
an omen of intrusion
from beyond the spaces
that I can control
and manage

inevitably
I examine my heart

seeking
to update its status

whether new harm
has befallen

am I in love
again
or still *in abstentia*

aloof from beauty and wile

from desire
and need

startled
but
as yet
unharmed

no
it beats strongly still

I am reassured
as every *lub*
is followed by its partner
dup

and the situation
is no more
than the soot
that falls from chimneys

**is not yet
existential
in its nature**

elation (two times)

Slipped by the terrace

these thoughts
run
like water released
at the sharp twist
of a faucet

released
to conceal themselves
as they will
in a game of hide
and find

leap forth
to *surprise*

slip by
on the terrace
where I wander
lost

my own meditations
illuminated
like lightning
strike
in darkness

and I need
to seek
immediately
I need
to seek you out

to tell you
what I
now know

RESCUE AND REDEMPTION

you smile
benevolence
and let me know
that you know
already

and that the thought
has meaning

and that I
have meaning

I am elated
then

now

I am elated
fully

twice

too suddenly

Made a sudden leap

I play
with intuition

tamper
with my future days

I look ahead
I
like to know
what is coming

what
is coming

I make
a sudden leap
because
suddenly
I *do* know

and
I am upon a moment
that is still
to come

I can hold it
in my hands

hold it up
against
the light

keep it
in my pocket
until I'm ready

until
it
is ready

then
I can live it
because
I know it
and it will not hold
a surprise

I do not like
being surprised
by a moment
that leaps up on me
too
suddenly

watching the gold

And seeing that it was a soft October night

while the sun
takes time
to settle

and this
being such a soft night
for october

shall we walk
just
you and I

on the trail
up
to the vineyard

we can watch
to westward
as the changing light
turns the leaves
into
a kind of
gold

just as the grape
becomes
a wine

it will be
a sensual thing

almost
I would like
to touch the leaves

to feel the gold within them

RESCUE AND REDEMPTION

if we go
now
the sun
will take its time
to settle down

we can watch
the gold
become

used to be (then curled up)

Curled once about the house, and fell asleep

the evening news
rises up
to crowd around
the ceiling

think it came
from a fire
many miles away

the world outside
is alight

the bush
is blazing skyward

hearts
are burning
with every leaf
and twig
and branch
that dances flame

and it is all across
the nightly reportage

the reds
and yellows
violently seeking an escape
from behind the flat screen
where they
temporarily
dwell

the smoke
at bulletin end
curled around the room

curled round
and around
descending at last
to sleep
in a corner

I
do not sleep

I
cannot sleep

I see and feel
the visions
of what used
to be

as much as is needed

And indeed there will be time

though the light
is more
of evening
than the harsher hues
of midday
still
it remains

still
I can see

and though
the darkness
is less
a stranger
than once it was
well . . .

that is nothing

not really

there will be time
left
for you and I
to speak

time left to share
a body-shake
of laughter
even though
we end up in tears

holding each other

weeping
just a little
for what has been

but still
we both know
there is a lifetime
in a look

eternity
in silence
that lasts just as long
as we need

we've said it all
many times
and there is no joy
in being mundane
now

there will be time
for that
no shortage

after

we did some things
you and I
we did
do those things
didn't we

I would not want
to do them
again

but
there is pleasure
in having time left
to remember

do you recall . . .

I know
that you do

and you

you

know
now
that I do
too

back (into grey)

For the yellow smoke that slides along the street

the fog rolls in
through the streets
of my town

the shade
shifts
from black night
into grey

and my feet
sound

clear
beneath the shroud

.
.
.

closer
to a streetlight
colour
lives

suddenly
it is yellow smoke
that slides

into
a bus shelter

across
the slatted rest
of a curb-side seat

dancing
in the damp
fogged motes
of warm light

until I fade
clarity
by clarity

pace by pace

back into a grey shade
then
to night

well done (the day)

Rubbing its back upon the window-panes

it is a day
filled with light
from
first dawn

all through its hours
no cloud
no doubt

and in the afternoon
coming on
to evening

it rubs its back
job done
against a window pane

I have been riveted
just watching

being

as another day
unfolded

little tears
and little dramas

minute triumphs
and small pains

the day
is done
and the job
is done

all
is done
quite well

for everything

There will be time, there will be time

wait

the season
will change

see
even now
the tree
is emerging

flowers come

as clouds
drift by

your last thought
is gone
succeeded
by the coming one

a day starts

another
ends

whatever
is to be next

there will be
time

there will
be time

for being
you
for being new
for being
too
for you
and me
enough to see
time
to feel . . .

free

time
time
time
time

there will be

time
time
time
time

enough

white face (and rhyme)

To prepare a face to meet the faces that you meet

mirror you
and mirror
me

take the paste
and slather

make a moue
amid
the lather

smooth it down
pat-a-cake
slap it slip
into
a face-like shape

mould your visage
as I do
mine

meet my true face
first grin
in line

then
turn around
your courage built
to meet
the faces rushing

rushing

on
the street

hold your head
up
you are not alone

I'll hold
my head up
two
as one

and step in time
your step
with mine

we mime we mime
two clowns
silently
in rhyme

novel advice (my darlings)

There will be time to murder and create

always kill
your darlings

sage advice
for one and all

you need
to kill your darlings
but . . .

all in time

you can take it
slow

first
build them up
with
all your heart

make them ring clearly
sound
and true

make them
loveable

likeable
and hateful
both

essential

critical

unimaginable

make of them
the pumping heart

that reveals the story
with each beat

take your time
write
what you want
and then . . .

and then . . .

commit a little mayhem

don't hesitate
to dramatize

let chaos rule
throughout
the world

always
the way you guide

and no need to explain
your *why*
to anyone

why did you
kill
our darlings

why not keep them

were they not
good

we all feel
so
vulnerable
with our darlings
gone

and wonder

we wonder

what will happen
to us
in the chapter
that you write
next

time and hands (in the river)

And time for all the works and days of hands

say
to the river
there is time

say to the breezes
there is time

say it to the sky
shout it
toward heaven

for all
who can hear
there is time

time
to remember
all the wrongs
*(yea
all the rights)*

time to take
a moment
of reflection

time enough
for everything

for the work of these
my hands

there is time

if there is daylight
there is time

don't I know
the hourglass
is pouring sand
(my sand
yes
I do)

don't I know
each moment
is a pearl
(I know
I know
it is true)

don't you think I know
the hour
is coming
(here it is
oh
here
it is)

I know
but
for me
there still seems
time

time is a circle
I
am rounding

time
is ninety degrees
in the corner
of a square

RESCUE AND REDEMPTION

I will come
to where I started
I will be
the way
that I was
then

and the time
for these hands
to be working
will be done

holding on (to questions)

That lift and drop a question on your plate

and
are we not
at the end
of times

you and I

we spend hours
in contemplation

self

other

out there

within

and all the ways
of thought
and wonder
lead
toward conclusion

the search for answers
results
in questions
dropped squalling
as though from the wide blue

as though
from the heart
of storm

from nether regions
not visited
but dreamt

the end of times
my apocalypse-o

we should pack
all our bags
and baggage

but
I look at you
and wonder
again

where

where for you

where
for me

.
.
.

take my hand

forget all that
and take my hand

until the end

let us
hold

ocean (time)

Time for you and time for me

it is
a river

running from somewhere
that was
the start

it is a flow
that washes
by the place
my feet have found

it is a silver line
leading
into the distance
until it fades

and somewhere
far enough
ahead
that I cannot see

it is the ocean

waiting patient
until I become
as one
with the waving
of a tide
that ebbs
and flows

yet
there is time
enough
for all that I must do

and
there is time enough
I think
for you to do what you must do
as well

time enough
to join the river
and to twirl
a while
in idled eddies
on the way

until the sea of time
brings us
to ocean side

that great repository
of everything
that is that was
that
could have been

one day

soon enough

no hurry

time

of rock pools (and responses)

And time yet for a hundred indecisions

it is the case
that . . .

oh
I don't know

I find myself
in situations

and the splash
of softened water
in the confines
of the pool
brings me
acutely
to the knowledge
of another

I realise
again
that there are points
beyond returning

and a question hovers
just there
beyond my reach

do I allow
the hand that
even now
is seeking purchase
in the vicinity
of my knee

prelude to love
perhaps
down
among the suds

to the quiet
rhythmic pulse
of an electric motor

making bubbles
swirl
while concealing traces
minimal

suggestions
that are a naked body
at full languish

time

time

to rise
or to recede

as the tide
alternately exposes
and then subsumes
the eager pools
carved
spa-like
along a rocky shore

eagerness
yes

eagerness yes yes
but . . .

oh
a first touch
that is a fingertip
that is
a shiver

exploring
through the froth

**seeking
an urgency
in the answer
to a question**

you and me (at three o'clock)

And for a hundred visions and revisions

three o'clock
is a patter
of rain
and memories

moving pictures
in the theatre
of the mind

sometimes
it seems the past
is a treasure house
of moments lost

of choices taken
now subject
to revision

it has been
a long journey
this

filled
with instances of you
and me

the you
has sometimes
come and gone

different faces
temporarily in situ

the me
always the same

no matter how
different
always the same

trying hard

eternally striving

reaching with such
intense
endeavour

while erring
in recurrent patterns

minutely changed
with each new occasion
of you

your every
incarnation

at three o'clock
sometimes
a different
same old
situation
comes alive
again

playing
in the theatre
that reels inside
my head

and I know
the ways
I could have changed
the outcomes

but

tcha

tcha

what point
when
here we are

this moment
now
this
you
and this me

while three o'clock
is only ancient visions
played
with an impoverished
recall

out
my light

out
right now

I wish
to sleep

a breakfast taken (deshabille)

Before the taking of a toast and tea

it becomes
a breakfast
taken in your bed

a straightening
of sheets
before the toast

two pieces
for me

and nothing said
of
the deshabille
that decorates
the corners

memories
of the night
that is now
gone

coffee
to damp down
stale breath

a question
suspended
in the air

a glance across
to determine
if
all is well
in aftermath

a half-embarrassed
chuckle
emerges reluctantly
at a vivid memory
flashing past

another glance

another question

tentative
a hand
and
an unexpected
electricity

the toast
is crumbs
abandoned

the coffee
cold
a brown mark left
upon the cup

becomes
a breakfast

taken
in your bed

the dregs say (it is time)

In the room the women come and go

the courtesan
today
has put her time
in

coffee now

a short black
is all the time left
on this roster

a finger
touches make-up
but
not important
anymore

there is no longer thought
of customers
come and gone
and
come
and gone again

a little drop
of something
to flavour
the caffeine

a chat
about a child
and school
and mortgages
with a colleague

street clothes
in the lounge
while negligees
drift by

leading charcoal suits
that come
before they go

read the dregs
left to run
down the sides
of an upturned cup

search
for coffee words
and symbols
meaning . . .

nothing there
but broken paths
uncertain runs
and rivulets

little signs that say

*it's time
to go home*

more (the same) like you

Talking of Michelangelo

what I am
from
what I've been

every breath
taken in
has changed me

words
that I have spoken

and
tears I shed
in anguish

what is
I
is now
not
what *I* once was

a sculpture
that
reshapes
at every blinking
of an eye

and I shape
myself
a little more
like you

as we walk out
together
the length
of my step
is changed

the thoughts
that I allow
to represent me

the stature
I assign
to who
I believe I am

a little more
like you

a little more
the same

RESCUE AND REDEMPTION

original project response

My initial response and submission (written for the original project in around 2001) was the poem no, *not the old city* which I have included below. It will be easy for a reader to identify it as work from an earlier phase of my writing career.

no not the old city

Streets that follow like a tedious argument

and the old city is a wasting of time   there is nothing of value there
no return on that investment   those twenty years of purgatude
spent with an aspirational heart   every day   from the beginning
when to walk that way was something fresh and new   each pace
holding its own speed and reason   much like here perhaps
here   in this newer place   with this newer purpose
so draped with the coatings   now   of experience knowledge
perhaps it is not the purpose that has changed   not so very much

this though   this is not that ancient wreckage   with its labyrinth byways
foetid distractions   those twisted streets that follow like a tedious argument
renewed afresh upon boulevards and avenues that open yawning black
in sickly   honeyed   invitation with each tempted visitation to that past   no
this is newer ground   these paths are fresh and open
look up
that blue is the sky   in this place it is mine   yours
ours   if you wish it
you and me   and the coloured blue of our own sky

no   let us not go near to the old city
there is nothing there for us   nothing

source materials

If you would like to find some information about T. S. Eliot, his life and his writing, a good place to start is his entry in Wikipedia: https://en.wikipedia.org/wiki/T._S._Eliot

I have accessed the source poems for this project from the following online locations:

The Reader (Lowell): https://www.thereader.org.uk/featured-poem-madonna-of-the-evening-flowers-by-amy-lowell/

The Walt Whitman Archive (Whitman): https://whitmanarchive.org/published/LG/

The Poetry Foundation (T. S. Eliot): https://www.poetryfoundation.org/poetrymagazine/poems/44212/the-love-song-of-j-alfred-prufrock

The translation from the latin for the opening lines was sourced from Wikipedia: https://en.wikipedia.org/wiki/The_Love_Song_of_J._Alfred_Prufrock

I commend these organisations, and the work of the selected poets to you.

If you would like to find some information about T. S. Eliot, his life and his writing, a good place to start is his entry in Wikipedia: https://en.wikipedia.org/wiki/T._S._Eliot

I have accessed the source poems for this project from the following online locations:

The Reader (Lowell): https://www.thereader.org.uk/featured-poem-madonna-of-the-evening-flowers-by-amy-lowell/

The Walt Whitman Archive (Whitman): https://whitmanarchive.org/published/LG/

The Poetry Foundation (T. S. Eliot): https://www.poetryfoundation.org/poetrymagazine/poems/44212/the-love-song-of-j-alfred-prufrock

FP, 2020

RESCUE AND REDEMPTION

author information

About Frank Prem

Frank Prem has been a storytelling poet since his teenage years. He has been a psychiatric nurse through all of his professional career, which now exceeds forty years.

He has been published in magazines, online zines and anthologies in Australia, and in a number of other countries, and has both performed and recorded his work as spoken word.

He lives with his wife in the beautiful township of Beechworth in North East Victoria, Australia.

Connect with Frank

As the author, I hope you enjoyed *Walk Away Silver Heart*. I think that mine is a unique style of writing that can appeal beyond a *'pure poetry'* readership.

If you enjoyed it, I'd like to ask you to do two small things for me.

First, take a moment to leave a short review of this book on Amazon by visiting **mybook.to/Rescue_and_Redemption** and clicking on the button (near the bottom of the page) that is labelled "Write a customer review."

Online reviews provide social proof to readers and are critical to Indie authors such as myself.

The second thing is, please pop over to my Author Webpage at **https://FrankPrem.com** and sign up to join my Newsletter list. From time to time I'll let you know what is happening with myself and my writing, as well as keeping you informed of any giveaways I may be planning.

My full list of contacts are below. Don't hesitate to get in touch.

Home Page:
FrankPrem.com

Amazon Author Page:
https://www.amazon.com/-/e/B07L61HNZ4

Goodreads Author Page:
https://www.goodreads.com/author/show/18679262.Frank_Prem

Facebook page:
https://www.facebook.com/frankprem2

YouTube Channel:
https://www.youtube.com/channel/UCvfW2WowqY1euOCj76LDKg

Twitter:
https://twitter.com/frank_prem

coming soon

Walk Away Silver Heart

Part 1 of **A Love Poetry Trilogy** is *walk away silver heart*, and features love poems inspired by Amy Lowell's *Madonna of the Evening Flowers*.

ISBN: 978-1-925963-06-9 (pbk)
ISBN 978-1-925963-01-4 (e-bk)

A Kiss For The Worthy

Part 2 of **A Love Poetry Trilogy** is *a kiss for the worthy* and features love poems inspired by Walt Whitman's *Song of myself (Leaves of Grass)*.

ISBN 978-1-925963-04-5 (pbk)
ISBN 978-1-925963-05-2 (e-bk)

other published works

Frank Prem

Small Town Kid (2018)
ISBN: 978-0-9751442-3-7 (pbk)
ISBN: 978-0-9751442-4-4 (e-bk)

Devil In The Wind (2019)
ISBN: 978-0-9751442-6-8 (pbk)
ISBN: 978-0-9751442-7-5 (e-bk)

The New Asylum (2019)
ISBN: 978-0-9751442-8-2 (pbk)
ISBN: 978-0-9751442-5-1 (e-bk)

With Other Authors

Herja, Devastation - With Cage Dunn (2019)
ISBN: 978-1-925905-04-5 (pbk)
ISBN: 978-1-925905-03-8 (e-bk)

Short Stories of Forest and Fantasy: Fantasy Anthology by OzTales(2019)
ISBN: 978-0-9872863-7-6 (pbk)
ISBN: 978-0-9872863-5-2 (e-bk)

Aquarius: Speculative Fiction Inspired by the Zodiac (The Zodiac Series) by Deadset Press
ISBN: 978-1393586371 (pbk)

what readers say

Small Town Kid

A modern-day minstrel

As a 'New Australian' of eastern European heritage, much of Frenki's life resonates with me, and yet it's the imagery of time and place that makes these poems familiar to all Australians. And perhaps to non-Australians as well. Boyhood and the wonder years. Some things are universal. Highly recommended

—A. F. (Australia)

Small-Town Kid is a wonderful collection
With so few words Frank is able to paint a picture so vivid you can't help but get lost in the story. Whether he's talking about family, a picnic, a trip to the butcher or even the outside toilet it's difficult not become immersed in the words and imagine yourself right there with him. Cover to cover, this is an excellent read.

—S. T. (Australia)

A poet's walk through his childhood in a small Australian town. From the dedication poem, 'I Can Hardly Wait to Show You', to 'Circular Square Town', Frank Prem's chronological journey from infancy to the present has a familiar feel to it, almost as if you were taking a walk through your own memory lane to recall the innumerable small, but unforgettable moments that make up a life.

—J. L. (USA)

Devil In The Wind

I live in the US, and though I recall these fires, I never knew the personal stories behind them. Frank Prem instantly grips you by the throat in his step-by-step story of survival.
I was especially taken because he told the story through poetry, which I've never related to this way. It was stark and vivid, the language of a survivor. It's a quick read, but trust me, this book will stay with you.

Bravo!

—K. K. (USA)

Very moving, beautiful, and terrible

—J. S. (South Africa)

Outstanding!
I'm not normally a reader of poetry, but Devil in the Wind captured the essence of 7 February 2009, and the days and weeks afterwards, with eloquence and ease. Beautifully written, the author has given a human voice to those who matter. Highly recommended.

—B. T. (Australia)

The New Asylum

Brilliant succinct memoir. These insightful, thought provoking behind-the-scene stories are woven so seamlessly you'll lose track of time. 'this somebody's boy' is one of many which will hold your heart.

__M.P-B. (Australia)

Words can't do justice to the emotional journey I travelled in (reading this collection). I don't think anything can. My heart bled, my eyes burned. And I will read it again, to remind me.

__C. D. (Australia)

"The eternal asylums of mental health ...another shift in the backwards."
If I had to pick one book over the past year that has truly resonated with me, this would be it. It's a hauntingly beautiful window into the successes and failures of working with the mentally disabled, and the impact on the human psyche.

__K. B. (USA)

Herja, Devastation

How does a reader give this work the credit it deserves? Simply written, powerfully felt. A man with a job, a woman he loves beyond sanity (or is it his only hold on sanity?).
He is her tool, he says, and I feel the depth of that longing to be nothing more than that. Loved it. Can't say that enough.

__C. (Australia)

The cover alone was enough to excite me to look inside. I'm glad I did.
I loved this book. I don't know whether to call it poetry or prose, and I'd never heard of Eddic tales, but if that's your thing, or you want to feel the subtle menace, albeit from a loving hand.
This is a book I will reread and remember for a long, long time.

__C. (Australia)

As a combination of poetry, prose, and wonderfully ominous illustrations, I found Herja, Devastation refreshingly original. The narrative slipped seamlessly between the two forms and the valkyrie/assassin story carried my interest throughout. Highly recommended!

—G. B. (Australia)

FrankPrem.com

www.ingramcontent.com/pod-product-compliance
Lightning Source LLC
Chambersburg PA
CBHW052025290426
44112CB00014B/2388